Tips and Tricks for Stress-Free Downsizing

A Step by Step Guide to Moving On

Kay Newton

Praise For Tips and Tricks for Stress-Free Downsizing

"This book is full of excellent practical advice, as well as warmth and recognition of the emotional side of downsizing. The step by step guide and your tips were clear, sensible and very workable. There are plenty of books about decluttering and living with less, but you write from the heart, and from real-life experience, not because it's the latest trend or because you're jumping on a bandwagon. This shines through in every aspect of the book. I had to downsize a couple of years ago and it wasn't something I wanted to do, so it was a very tough process for me personally. I wish I'd had your book to refer to at the time. I think it would have made the whole process far less painful. Even after the fact, I've found some help from reading this, so thank you."

Andrea Steel, UK

"Wow! This really hits home the fact that we hang on to and carry so much STUFF around with us that is really just baggage!
It is really all about change, and that can be the most uncomfortable thing to do.
By asking the questions Kay highlights the issue, and using the tips suggested can clarify the reasons for doing it - which makes it easier to do.

A great little companion to have when the time comes to downsize.
Thank you Kay."

Linda Ledwidge, Spain

"I so get this little book, yet I failed to do the last step when I downsized and I now know it would have made such a big difference to how I settled into my new home. I am going to recommend this to others."

Michelle Lupec, USA

With Thanks

I am grateful to Ian and Vanessa from Greenwave Promotions, who have been on an editing journey with me for the past few years, nudging me further down the road to greatness.

To Marie Tillbert for the awesome book cover design.

To all my peeps who keep me motivated and get me out of bed in the morning with positive words of encouragement and inspirational stories.

And finally to the four men in my life. I love them very much: James, Max, Tom and Steven.

About

Kay is an award-winning international speaker, enthusiastic author, blogger, artist and Midlife Stress Buster. Her clients love her straight talking and practical stress-relieving holistic help and support.
Kay's books include:

How to Clean Your Home Organically - De-Stress Your Surroundings

The Art of Midlife Stress Busting - Seven Steps to Declutter Your Mind Without Pills or Potions

She co-authored the ebooks in the *Quick Fix For* series, and is a contributing author to *Hot Women Rock* and *A Journey of Riches*.

Kay hails from Leeds in Yorkshire, England. In her early 20s, she jumped on board a 'gin palace' leaving Hull for sunnier shores in Spain, and refused to swim back. She set up her own business looking after holiday homes for the rich and famous, became an eco-landlady extraordinaire, and the mother of two boys. She has been married for over 25 years.

In 2015, after a 30-year dream life on the Spanish island of Mallorca, Kay and her husband decided that rather than having an empty nest, they preferred 'no nest'. Leaving their two grown boys to fend for themselves, they decluttered and downsized to a two-roomed house with a tin roof next to a pristine beach on the island of Zanzibar, off the coast of Tanzania. Kay now lives a life free of unnecessary stress, and has never been happier.

Beachcombing one day, she decided it's time to focus on ridding the Boomer generation of unnecessary stress. She founded the Midlife Virtual Retreat, an online session to relax, rejuvenate and have fun.
You can join her here:
https://www.facebook.com/TheMidlifeStressBuster/

You can also find Kay Newton The Midlife Stress Buster here:
https://www.kay-newton.com/

Table of Contents

Foreword

Stress is considered a leading cause of death in people over 50. Midlifers have a lot to deal with: ageing parents, empty nests, boomerang kids, worries over pension shortfalls, mortgages or health care plans, caregiving, the loss of a loved one, ill health, divorce, moving home, loneliness, isolation - the list seems endless.

In the US alone, 1 in 10 people over the age of 45 are thought to suffer from stress-related anxiety and depression. Worries about money, work, politics, the economy, relationships, health, and personal and national security are cited as causes (https://www.apa.org/news/press/releases/stress/2011/final-2011.pdf).

Many at midlife feel stressed, trapped in a downward spiral they can't escape. It's said that women suffer from stress more than men. The constant need to consume and hoard, and a tendency to live amongst clutter also contributes to stress. A sedentary lifestyle and unhealthy eating habits add their two-penn'orth to a general feeling of dissatisfaction with our lives.

The medical profession treats stress and anxiety by prescribing anti-depressants, which in turn cause other health issues. The good news is that with a little work midlifers can glide gracefully into old age, feeling calmer and more content, while embracing the concept of being *Sensibly Selfish*.

Sensibly Selfish is all about giving yourself permission to be the first priority, for the highest good. When you put yourself first, you can focus on your own well-being, and thus be in the right place energetically to be able to help others. Just like in the aircraft emergency protocol, you have to put on your own oxygen mask before you can help others.

Introduction - My Story

Over the past five years I have downsized twice, once to leave our four-bedroomed home and move a few metres away, to our converted barn. My husband and I did this when our two boys left the nest. It enabled us to rent out the bigger house to summer guests, creating more income.

Then, in 2015 my husband and I moved from our home in Mallorca, Spain, where we had lived for 30 years, to live in a two-roomed house in Zanzibar, Tanzania, 11 hours by plane and over 9000km away, with just two suitcases of 20kg each. We left our luxurious lifestyle behind, as well as our two grown boys. We now live within five minutes of the most pristine exotic beach, and we have never been happier.

By nature I'm an organised person, so when tackling a job such as downsizing I immediately break the task down into bite-sized chunks. I can see what the next stage will be and what issues will be faced. And that's how this book is laid out for you - step by step. It will tell you what you need to do before you even lift a finger, how the actual downsizing is best tackled and what to do when all is finished.

So let's begin...

The Very First Steps

"Be as simple as you can be; you will be astonished to see how uncomplicated and happy your life can become." Paramahasa Yogonada

The hardest part about downsizing is the time it takes. Planning and organisation become key elements in the process. The earlier you start to sort your stuff, the easier it will be.

By downsizing, you are going to change your life. There will be things you can't take with you. You may need to let go of these items and for some, this may be a difficult process. Step by step is the only way to move forward.

As with any life-changing process, before you begin it's well worth sitting with pen and paper for a while. It's important to be confident that you are moving home for the right reasons. For this stage, set aside time in your diary and sit somewhere quiet with a pen, paper or journal. Time spent here will save you a lot of stress later.

Use the ten questions below to help you write down your thoughts and feelings about downsizing. You may like to ignore some and you may like to add others – it's up to you.

Tip: the aim is not to focus on blame, judgement or criticism of your circumstances. It is about transferring your thoughts onto paper so that you can use them later to positive effect. I call it 'thought vomiting'! Just put your thoughts onto paper, simples.

When you have answered all the questions, close your book and leave it for 24 hours. Then and only then, if you wish, you can come back to edit the thoughts you wrote down. You may not feel a need to change anything you wrote. We will talk about this in a moment.

1. Why Am I Downsizing?

This question needs time and patience - a one-line answer won't do. You can brainstorm this and write down all the reasons as they come into your head (you might have 20 on the page by the time you've finished), or you can ask yourself the following <u>at least</u> 10 times:

"My reason for downsizing is……*(fill in the blank)*…….?" (repeat).

You can also use both approaches.

Doing this process often leads to the real reason you are downsizing. For example, I had originally thought my true reason for downsizing was economic, though I used to joke it was also so that I wouldn't have to deal with boomerang kids because there would be no space for them. However, when I asked myself this question and repeated it 10 times, it emerged that my reason had more to do with death.

I didn't want others to have to sort through all my accumulated stuff when I am gone, as I had done for a friend when she died alone aged 85. Then again, two years later, I dealt with my parents' home, the house where I grew up, and where they had lived for 55 years. It was after these experiences that I vowed I never wanted my kids to have to do the same.

Other reasons people give include: making a fresh start; less cleaning; reduced stress; better cash flow; more time; easier upkeep; getting rid of an 'empty nest' after the children have left; simpler maintenance; having a community of like-minded neighbours; special services, such as meals, transportation, a clubhouse, and planned activities; saving money; having no stairs; or moving to a more suitable climate.

If your reason isn't your choice, for example ill health, or you lost your job and can't pay the mortgage, include how this makes you feel in your answer. Remember, at this stage it's just about transferring your thoughts onto paper; there are no right or wrong answers.

Doing this work and becoming aware of the true reason you are downsizing will enable you to live your new life as if you are already in your new space right now. So when you do move, it will feel familiar.

Tip: you shouldn't be downsizing because you feel it's the trendy thing to do, or just because everyone today believes less is more (unless of course you believe that too). Living in a tiny home may come with its own stresses; why not rent for a while or take a holiday in a smaller space before you commit to making it a permanent lifestyle.

2. What Will It Mean To Live In A Smaller Space?

Think about what it will mean to live in a smaller space. This is an opportunity to look at the reasons you uncovered in answering Question One, and elaborate on what it will mean to you to live in your new home.

Imagine sitting in your new space: the move has been made, your things have been positioned and your new life is about to begin. What will this mean?

Go into as much detail as possible, in order to make it feel as if it has already happened.

Write until you can write no more. For example:

I will feel happy and content in my new home, my to-do list is short. I now have so much 'me' time I can choose to spend my time writing and painting using my vivid, colourful imagination. I can exercise until my heart sings and go for a leisurely walk on the beach, enjoying the warmth of the sun, smelling the salty ocean and chatting to the local people.

3. What Will My New Space Look and Feel Like?

Now that you know how you will feel, imagine yourself actually moving around your new home, touching your personal items as you walk around, taking in the smell as you pass the kitchen, and looking out of the window. What can you see and hear? Use all your senses to imagine your new life in this space. Ask yourself...

How will I feel?
What will I see?
What will I hear?
What will I taste?
What will I touch?

Keep writing and make notes until you have imagined every part of your new home in and out. For example:

My morning will begin by an awareness of the smell of newness in my bedroom and the crispness of the new white sheets on my bed. As the sun enters the room and touches my cheek I will become aware of the chirping birds outside the window and I will hear the clock chime downstairs. A quick stretch and I am happy to jump out of bed, touching the shiny wooden handrail on the stairs as I head for the kitchen to make a pot of coffee...

This exercise is also good to create thoughts on where exactly you're going to put a painting you cherish so much, or what you might put in that possible awkward corner in your new home, which needs an object or piece of furniture, yet right now, you are unsure what. Let your mind wander and make notes as you go along. This will save you time later.

4. What Will I Keep and What Has To Go?
Now, in your mind's eye you have walked around you new home with your furniture installed, and you may have realised that some of the larger pieces of furniture you currently own will not fit into your new space.

Write down the pieces that you know will fit, so when you come to move you already know with confidence what you are keeping and what has to go. This will make you more time efficient later.

Tip: not everyone can see with their mind's eye. If this applies to you don't worry, it's normal. You can sit with a physical plan of your new space and make scaled images of your furniture out of cardboard. Move them around until you know where they will go. Then you can mark these items on the plan and later you can put stickers on each item of furniture so you know they have been allocated a space in your new home.

Tip: when doing this exercise remember to allow for fitting items through door frames! For example, we once bought a double bed with a double frame that wouldn't go up the stairs, so we ended up putting the base in another room and sleeping on the mattress on the floor until two new single bases could be bought that would fit.

On a personal note, on our last downsize my husband and I decided to leave all our furniture in the old house. The reason was that each piece was chosen for that particular house, and looked right in its current space. It wouldn't look right in our new environment. Also, it would have cost too much to get it to Zanzibar and we would have had difficulty choosing just a few pieces to fit our two-roomed home here. Anyway, by now it would have all been eaten by the vicious African bugs!

Tip: think about the storage space you will need in your new home. Downsizing means less space, so you may have to find new ways to use space effectively. Most people overestimate exactly how much storage space they will have in their new home.

5. Which Items Are Going To Cause Me The Most Pain?

You may feel emotionally attached to some items. The memories associated with items can be very strong; we may feel uncomfortable just thinking about them. Now is the time to list these items on a separate page so that you can deal with them.

When you have a list, you may decide you need help to work through these emotional attachments. It's normal to feel attached to items, and it's ok to ask for help (see 6 below).

Tip: think about alternative ways you can overcome the emotions that arise when you think of possibly letting certain things go . Can you make a small book of photos and thoughts as a keepsake, instead of keeping the actual item? Can you pass these treasured items onto other members of the family? Think about ways you can let go of them, in order to lessen the pain before you even start the process.

6. Who Can Help?

Friends, family or professionals may help you to overcome emotional hurdles. Who else can help you with other tasks? This is not something to tackle alone. Downsizing is physically and mentally tiring, and stressful. Having the right support is important for your success. List all the people you think might help. It might be a professional company which helps you downsize; a removal company who come and help pack and then move your items to your new home; a caring friend who makes cups of tea for you and guides you in your decisions; a family member who is happy to rehouse furniture in their home; or perhaps a local charity which is only too happy to come and remove items for free.

Check the local telephone directory to see what's available in your area - you may be surprised how much help is out there. Don't be afraid to ask; the worst you will get is a 'no', and you'll probably hear 'yes' many times. Get professional local help, either recommended by a friend, family member or health practitioner.

Make your list now, so you know who you can call upon. Later, you can work with this list to finalise it and find important contact details. Just jot thoughts down for now. Add anyone and everyone to your list. Many hands certainly make light work when it comes to downsizing.

7. What Do I Really Need?

Look around your home and assess what you need to keep. It probably won't be as much as you think. I managed to pack all my needs; clothes, shoes, toiletries, paperwork and electrical goods into a 20kg suitcase! After 12 months here in Zanzibar, I now feel that even 20kgs are too much. Why not make a list of the items that would fit into your suitcase?

These are the items you will take with you, no matter what. Now look around your current home with this in mind. Do you have items that you use occasionally, less than once a year for example? Let go of them. You can always rent or borrow if you need them in the future.

8. How Will I Get Rid of My Unwanted Items?

This is a fab question to ask - and it includes the question *when* will I get rid of my unwanted items?

Think about where you want your unwanted items to go: friends, charity shops (they will need to collect or you to deliver), the recycling centre. You may want to hold a garage or car boot sale, sell on eBay or at a local auction.

Whichever method(s) you choose, you will need to plan in advance, and put dates into a diary so that it happens. Take time now to list the hows and whens. Later, you can add the contact information for each person and finalise dates.

9. What Storage Will I Need?

As mentioned earlier, most people underestimate the storage space they require, so it's time to think about what methods and systems you have for storing items in your new home. If space is tight, smart new storage systems will make things more efficient.

Make a list of any boxes and other storage systems that you need to buy for your new home. Will buying these now and filling them with your items help with the moving process? (It will certainly make for less work when you get there, because you won't need to transfer things after your move.) If the answer is yes, then put a list together and set aside time to purchase them.

Tip: if you can avoid external storage, do so; you will be charged every month. The cost of the storage unit will almost invariably be more than the items stored, unless you're well-organised and can plan to get rid of stored items by a set date, for example within 12 months.

10. What Other Things Do I Need For My Move?

What else will help your downsizing go smoothly? After answering all the questions above, this one will help make sure you're ready to focus on the task ahead. Do you need to buy bin bags, storage boxes, tape, *coloured stickers or marker pens? Who do you need to contact? Perhaps a hire company or a friend? Use their feedback to confirm that you are on the right track.

Tip: coloured stickers are a great thing to have when preparing to move - you can place them on items and create a code system which will save a lot of time on the day. For example, green stickered furniture will go to the new home, while red stickers need re-housing.

A blue stickered box will go to the new bathroom, and a yellow box will go to the new kitchen.

Tip: *check out my Pinterest boards for ecoliving, decluttering and storage ideas. You can find the links to Pinterest at the end of this book.*

Now you have answered all 10 questions, close your book and come back to it in 24 hours.

24 hours later

After 24 hours you can sit quietly and read what you have written. Does it sound exciting and positive, or does it feel daunting and negative? How can you rephrase any negative thoughts so they sound more positive? Once you have rephrased the negative words, highlight or underline all the positive words with you find. Writing down positive words will help keep you focused throughout the process, and make it more enjoyable.

Words you may like to use: excitement, new start, choice, appreciate, awakening, beauty, calm, creative, dream, deserve, fantastic. If you are stuck for more positive word ideas, check out the resource section for a link to *the positive words* website.

Go through your notes for the previous nine questions and add any contact information that is missing, and any new thoughts that have come to you over the last

24 hours. Make your shopping lists ready to buy your storage items and any extras you need.

Using Your Written Work

Take the notes you have from answering the ten questions above and re-read them. Find one word or phrase that really captures your reason for downsizing. This word or phrase will become your mantra, so when you hesitate over an object you can chant your mantra in order to refocus. This will help keep the work moving forward, saving time and energy. For example, your word might be Happy, New, Less is More, Me-Time, Sassy Space, Haven, or whatever you choose.

To Recap

Before you begin the downsizing process, sit with pen and paper, look at the reasons you are downsizing, and ask yourself:

Why am I downsizing?
What will it mean to live in a smaller space?
What will my new space look and feel like?
What will I keep and what has to go?
Which items are going to cause me the most pain?
Who can help me?
What do I really need?
How will I get rid of my unwanted items?
Do I need to think about storage?

What other things do I need for my move?

Take a look at your answers 24 hours later, add missing items and contact details and choose your positive mantra to see you through the process.

When you know the answers to these questions, you'll find you have the right attitude to speed up the downsizing process and make sure you feel happy and confident in your new surroundings.

Tip: write down your mantra now and place it where you can see it daily.

Now you're ready to begin downsizing.

The Process of Downsizing

"Have nothing in your house that you do not know to be useful or believe to be beautiful." William Morris

The process is very similar to the decluttering process outlined in *The Quick Fix For Decluttering* book, which you can buy on Amazon. (See the Resources section for information). There are five stages to downsizing.

1. Detailed Audit

Go through each room and storage space in a methodical manner. Work from the entrance door, going around the room from left to right. If you have a storage area or garage, take out everything that no longer serves you. Leave behind only things you want to keep. Be ruthless with things that you no longer use or that do not work, and clothes that don't fit, and place them in the appropriate piles below. The aim is to keep as much out of the landfill as possible:

Friends and family
Charity
Auction
On-line sale
Car boot
Recycling
Harmful

Tip: areas that may take longer are the kitchen, wardrobes, sheds, garages and paperwork. You may want to set these aside as separate jobs, allocating plenty of time to go through the contents.

Remove the unwanted items from your home as soon as possible. This not only saves time, it reduces stress.

2. Prune

Now that you have removed the first layer of unwanted items it's time to fine tune. It's rather like pruning a tree. First, you remove as much of the unwanted branches as you can, then you step back and take a look at the whole picture before doing a fine prune which gives shape to the final product.

Begin to audit your home in relation to your downsizing. Remove the larger furniture items that you will not be taking with you. Send them to their allotted pile.

Tip: old computers and hard drives. For security, take these to a certified shop to have the hard drive wiped clean.

Tip: paperwork - keep important documents in one file so they are on hand when you need them. Keep the paperwork required by the authorities where you live. Then make sure all other paper is either shredded or burned. Never place items with your name and *address or other important information into a normal rubbish bin.*

__Tip__: heirlooms and sentimental items - if you are handing these on to the next generation, you can take photographs, including ones of your old home, to preserve their memories.

3. Pack

Place the items you are going to move into boxes or their new storage place, ready for your new home. Colour code the boxes, for example, the bathroom could be blue, the kitchen yellow, the living room purple, and so on.

Pack your boxes so that heavier items are at the bottom. Think about packing boxes in relation to their need, for example: bathroom toiletries will probably be needed on the first night, spare towels will not. Pack your bathroom box with a toiletries bag and one towel on the top so you can find it easily.

__Tip__: as well as adding colour codes, mark each box with a number so you can unpack the most important boxes first.

__Tip__: If the contents of a box are fragile, mark the box accordingly. And after taping make sure you write 'This way up' on the box.

When I downsized from the main house to the guest house, I did every part of the house except the office. It had 20 years' paperwork in it and I knew it was going to be a huge job. I locked the room and for the first summer we rented out the house minus this area.

That winter, I packed everything into boxes and placed them on our bedroom floor. We just had space for two alleyways to each side of the bed and to the bathroom. It took me six months to clear out the contents box by box, yet I am so pleased I did it this way. If I had just stored it all, I would have had to deal with these boxes, as well as everything else when we moved to Zanzibar. I would not have had the time.

4. Move

When you begin to move into your new home, take the heavy objects first. There are two reasons: so you can make sure everything fits (without having to work around and stumble over smaller items on floor), and so you can use the items to store the contents of other boxes as they arrive. This saves time and effort. Put each colour-coded box in their respected areas as soon as you get them into the house, again to save time later.

Get help to move, it doesn't have to be paid help, offer tea and biscuits or a glass of wine and see who comes to your rescue! Moving on your own is stressful - it doesn't have to be hard.

5. Unpacking

Now you have everything in your new home. Don't be tempted to open all your boxes and begin rifling through for items. If you have followed the principles outlined above you will know where the important boxes are. Open these first and store their contents immediately. Open a box and store, open and store. This way you will organise as you go, saving time and energy.

Don't be surprised if you can't do it all in one day. Take your time and enjoy the process, there is no timescale.

To Recap
There are five stages of downsizing

- Detailed Audit
- Prune
- Pack
- Move
- Unpack

If you stick to the tips mentioned, the process will be relatively straightforward, even fun!

Congratulations. You have now downsized and moved into your new home. Now comes the most important part of the process, and a part which most people completely forget. Please read the next section carefully.

After Downsizing

"Own less. Live more." Unknown

So now you have downsized into your new living space and removed everything from the boxes. You are ready to start your new life. There is a vital step that many people forget. It has nothing to do with keeping a smaller space clean and tidy and clutter free, it's all to do with celebrating.

Celebrating anchors into your consciousness the fact that you have fully broken the ties with your old way of life. You are on a new path and starting a new journey. It's both exciting and daunting at the same time. Just like the process of downsizing, your new life begins with step by step action, and your first action is to celebrate.

By celebration, I am not talking about organising a house-warming party and inviting all your friends new and old, your family and even the removal guys to invade your new home - although that would be one way of cementing the fact that you have begun the next stage of your life!

Tip: If you are going to arrange a party, make sure you make a date in your diary that allows you to recover from the move first, so it doesn't leave you feeling exhausted. You choose the date, what your celebration will look like, and who will help you. Don't be bullied into doing something because others say you should.

What I am really talking about as a way of celebration is taking time out to get used to your new home, find things to be thankful for and celebrate your new space. A fabulous way to do this is with a smudge stick. Not sure what one is? Let me explain... a smudge stick is a bundle of dried herbs, usually sage, bound with string. The herbs are lit with a match and then the flame blown out to allow the smoke to do its cleansing work.

This small ritual or ceremony will allow you to focus on your new surroundings and make them your own. It's said that smudging can help combat negativity, clear the energy in your home and in your own energy field, and help you start anew. If you want to know more about smudging, then head over to www.Kay-Newton.com and look for the blog entitled Smudging Benefits. You can find the link in the Resources section at the end of this book.

If you're finding it hard to adjust to your new surroundings, revert to paper and pen and write down three things to be grateful for each morning, and each evening before going to bed. If you're still struggling after a few weeks, then seek professional help.

Tip: make a list of things that need improvement or alteration, and if necessary, get help to do these. For example, you may want to paint a wall a different colour or buy a new painting. The quicker you do these jobs, the more you will settle in, rather than the undone job settling on your shoulders and causing you mental anguish every time you pass by that area.

Tip: get out and about, get to know your new surroundings, and what's available within the local community. Find out where can you go to meet and make new friends. Get to know your community health practice or dentist, and so on.

To Recap

Celebrate your new home in a way that suits you. Get to know it inside and out. Perhaps smudge each room to energise them and yourself. Get to know your new community and surrounding area so that you can fit in quickly.

Thank You

Many thanks for reading to the end. I hope you found this book useful and have lots of new thoughts and ideas on how to go about downsizing. You now know what to do before you even move one item to your new home, how to make the move as stress-free as possible, and also why celebrating your transition is an essential part of the process.

Please feel free to share anything you have learned from your experience that is not mentioned in the book, or any inspirational story that can help someone else downsize effectively.

I'd love to hear from you: Kay(at)Kay-Newton.com

And Finally

Since you have reached the end of the book, I would like to offer you two FREE gifts:

Avoid 20 Household Items That Make You Unhappy

10 Floor Plan Mistakes and How to Avoid Them When Downsizing

The usual format for getting these free gifts is to sign up to an automated mailing list where I can then bombard you with yet more 'stuff' whenever I decide, which creates stress for both you and me. Stress for you, because your mail box will contain more than ever, and stress for me, because you probably won't bother to open them.

Therefore, I would rather do things the old-fashioned and personal way. Send an email to Kay(at)Kay-Kewton.com. Mark it 'Downsizing' and I will send the two FREE gifts direct to your inbox. Since this will be a personal message typed by my own fingers, please be patient. You may not receive an answer straight away if I am travelling (or if the internet in Zanzibar is playing up), and you may have to remind me again if I haven't answered within a week.

Kx

PS. I promise not to share your contact details with any third parties.

PPS. If you want to write back, that's up to you. I won't open up any further conversations with you, unless that's what you would like to do.

PPPS. Now you have moved to your new home it's time to focus on *you*. Head over to my website where you can download *The 5 Stress Myths You Need To Know Today* for FREE.

Resources

http://betterafter50.com/2015/11/downsizing-do-your-kids-want-your-crap/

http://www.housebeautiful.com/lifestyle/organizing-tips/advice/a3173/never-throw-out-when-downsizing/

Smudging Benefits:
https://www.kay-newton.com/smudge/

Positive words:
http://positivewordsresearch.com/list-of-positive-words/

Pinterest Boards:

https://es.pinterest.com/sensselfsecrets/decluttering-and-organizing/

To Find Kay:

Website: https://Kay-Newton.com
Facebook Page:
https://www.facebook.com/TheMidlifeStressBuster/
Facebook Group:
h t t p s : / / w w w . f a c e b o o k . c o m / g r o u p s /
MidlifeStressBusting

Kay's Other Books:

How to Clean Your Home Organically - De-Stress Your Surroundings

https://www.amazon.com/Clean-Your-Home-Organically-stress-ebook/dp/B071VH9YP3

The Art of Midlife Stress Busting – Seven Steps To Declutter Your Mind Without Pills Or Potions

https://www.amazon.com/Art-Midlife-Stress-Busting-Declutter-ebook/dp/B072862TVN

To buy titles in the Quick Fix Series by Pat Duckworth and Kay Newton:

amazon.com

Quick Fix For Empty Nest Syndrome -
http://amzn.to/2pNRl8x

Quick Fix For Parents Living With Boomerang Kids -
http://amzn.to/2pgxuM2

Quick Fix For Giving Glorious Gifts -
http://amzn.to/2pd570A

Quick Fix For Your Meaningful Midlife Relationship -
http://amzn.to/2pNqVSc

Quick Fix For Decluttering - http://amzn.to/2qzD8Nl

Quick Fix For Better Sleep - http://amzn.to/2qHCA5a

Printed in Great Britain
by Amazon

59416404R00030